Vanessa Kisuule's second release is a
It is a recipe book for personhooc
the seasons and the political clima
unspooling of long-harboured res
truths. It is a feverish fistful of r
instruction manual, a broken compass and an overheard conversation in the ladies' loo. It is at once a celebration of things to come and a mourning of things lost. It is a redefinition of what it is to be magical and otherworldly.

Vanessa Kisuule is a writer, performer, occasional burlesque artist and general empress of blag based in Bristol. She has won over ten slam titles including Farrago School's Out Slam Champion 2010, Bang Said the Gun Award, Poetry Rivals 2011, Next Generation Slam 2012, Slambassadors 2010, South West Hammer and Tongue Slam Champion 2012 and most recently the Roundhouse Slam 2014, Hammer and Tongue National Slam 2014 and the Nuyorican Poetry Slam in New York. She was the recipient of the Jerwood Micro Arts Bursary and the Leverhulme Arts Scholarship in 2017.

She has worked with the Southbank Centre, RADA, Warner Music and the Bristol City Council and has had her work featured on BBC iPlayer, BBC Radio 1, BBC Radio 4's *Woman's Hour*, the *Guardian*, *Huffington Post*, *Dazed & Confused*, *Blue Peter*, Sky TV and TEDx in Vienna. She represented the UK in two European Slam Championships in Sweden and Belgium, completed a ten-day tour around Germany in 2015 and spoke at the Global Forum of Migration and Development in Bangladesh in 2016. Her roster of international performances has extended in 2017 with invitations to Barcelona, Finland and Oslo. Her debut poetry collection *Joyriding the Storm* was published in April 2014 and her one-woman show *SEXY* toured in 2017/18 with the support of Arts Council England, Bristol Old Vic and Camden People's Theatre.

A Recipe for Sorcery

Vanessa Kisuule

Burning Eye

BurningEyeBooks
Never Knowingly
Mainstream

This edition published by Burning Eye Books 2017

www.burningeye.co.uk

@burningeyebooks

Burning Eye Books
15 West Hill, Portishead, BS20 6LG

ISBN 978 1 911570 19 6

A Recipe for Sorcery

these words are born from, inspired by and
gifted to women everywhere.
all other readers are welcome visitors.

Contents

a note on this book

the recipes included herein are not gluten-free, dairy-free, GMO-friendly or certified organic.
they are definitely not vegetarian.
if you're on a clean-eating, low-GI, low-carb, low-sugar or low-calorie regime then i regret to inform you that you have already taken in two hundred calories reading these first few sentences.

you should read labels more carefully, shouldn't you?

please do not fool yourself. to consume the inner workings of someone's mind is a form of cannibalism, a hunger both perverse and insatiable. if it's any consolation, you are not the only one with this affliction.

none of these words are fixed down because the assemblage process was a feverish one. if a verse spills into your lap or a line crumbles and lands in your tepid bath water, you are not entitled to a refund. don't consume these contents too quickly, else you run the risk of choking on loose sediment. any stray bits of crunch are likely to be fragments of teeth, bone or perhaps rubble from houses built from colonial brick and imperial bloodshed. it will taste unpleasant because it is exactly that.

unpleasant.

kind of like when your mum made you eat broccoli when all you wanted was to stuff your insolent mug with jam doughnuts and wotsits, these words may not always go down so easy. but you'll thank me later. or maybe you won't. but you won't know until later.

all that is left to say is that great pains have been taken to find an approximation of goodness in amongst the anguish and mayhem.

yes, goodness.

perhaps even unbridled joy. golly gosh.

so that's it, really.

how's about i stop telling you what to do now?

(bit tyrannical, isn't it? bit controlling.)

if you have any sense, you've never followed a recipe to the letter anyway.

so, all warnings aside, do what you must.

eat your fill.

an introduction to sorcery

i often dream of sorceress women
illuminated by restless firelight
all wearing different versions of my face

these crazy bitches squabble
over everything and nothing
they hold the blunt edge of the past
to each other's necks – threaten to slice

it is nothing less than
inevitable to watch them
split open like coconuts
an oddly tender excavation

examining all their fingers in turn
i do not even flinch at the blood, gristle
and ink cocktailing itself under their nails

look
they always say with contagious glee
look what we've found

a recipe for sustenance

you will need:

a consistent supply of cocoa butter

thick(er) skin

occasional spoonfuls of nostalgia, still warm. slightly fetid

money (if you can't find enough of this, replace with reserve helpings of agnostic prayer)

a bucket of saltwater fresh from the sea

olive oil that pours slow and tastes good enough to drink straight from the bottle

ten streetlit walks back home

rosé (not red. not white. *always* rosé)

a granny smith every day without fail

an army of books

someone's warmth against yours

a sharp needle and a sharp knife
(these both fix things in very different ways. choose wisely)

method:

we all need sustenance.

when you've eaten nothing but toast with the mould ripped from the corners, nothing but the candied styrofoam of empty email exchanges *(best wishes, regards, kind regards, warm regards, best, all the best)*, something happens to your insides. the pride flinches as if flayed with a whip christened in vinegar. it feels uniquely cruel to expose your thoughts to the light, so you hold them hostage inside you. it's a small wonder everything starts to snag.

but you are one of the lucky ones. all good things flower around you. even when your purse is empty and your ego flattened. even when the fridge is full of nothing but the gluey stains of food long since consumed.

you will learn to cook for yourself, far beyond the oven chips and cheese on toast you clung to when you were younger (though sometimes, even in this big girl body of yours, only greasy carbohydrates will do). possessive and trancelike in the kitchen, you will be quietly proud of how you ease into the actions of stirring, crushing and slicing. sponge cakes and brownies will mushroom out from their trays, a chemical reaction that will never cease to feel unlikely. miraculous.

you learn what feeds you.
what makes your stomach leaden.
what makes it resonate with the warm hum of a church bell.

there is no greater medicine than letting someone who cares for you cook for you. map their endearingly terrible posture as they hunch over the pots and pans. let your eyes blur over knife blades doing skittish jigs across chopping boards. this meal will taste richer – slow cooked in the patience that only people who have wiped your tears away with their own thumbs could have.

your bones need something to dance in. if some two-bit magician were to saw you in half, they could tell how deep your friendships were by the glow of your marrow, the beetroot syrup of your blood.

so when your body says *i'm hungry*
what it's saying is

we're not done here.

matooke beans and binyewa

it was a showdown
every dinner time
a mother's ill-fated attempts
to make the foreign
familiar

lack of elegance
assaulted the plate
ladled and heaped
into ungainly
mountains

bananas that weren't even sweet
a concrete sauce-brain-gunk
the beans were nothing like
their heinz-coloured cousin

parts of the meat still
clinging to bone and gristle
so loath to let go of its anchor

i had guiltless fantasies
of chips and pizza
neon-coloured juices
minstreling tropical scenes

the food sat defeated
my sombre cheeks
puffed full of righteousness
i did not like the taste
of this place where things
hung so heavy

a meal
submarined
to the bottom of the stomach
that couldn't be digested
broken down or absorbed

these days
i long for some sort of weight
a fierce belonging to a nationality
not borrowed or gifted
but simply mine

gnawing the raw flesh of the future
i often feel the past has abandoned me
it seems the bittersweetness of self
is an acquired taste

i should have filled my plate
whilst i still could

cornrows

hunched between my mother's knees
on sunday evenings
a wire forest of hair
submits to salt of stoic tear
hot gnash of plastic teeth

the hair was woven
into neat tracks of even plaits
i thought they were ugly
exposing taut conker-brown scalp
the skin always seemed seconds
from tearing

i did not sing into hairbrushes
all i had were wide-toothed combs
my hair did not do a pendulum
pop star swish from side to side

at school the girls ran paddle brushes
through their calm ocean tresses
i was the only one silencing a storm
each time i reached into my head

nevertheless
every week
my mother's hands were a steeple
repeat as many times as necessary
a kind god never gives you
more than you can handle

sometimes i want to run
back to the top of the stairs
settle myself back between her knees
where despite the searing pain
i felt safe and soft

and understood

a reminder for the sad brown girl you once were and sometimes still are

it is not either-or
my darling

it is not her
versus you

she is not a template
nor is she a mirror

all the years you squandered
thinking you were not enough

when all along
it was the words

the world that could not
hold the riot of your loveliness

that did not even know
where to begin

perhaps this is why you write
so language can finally quake

and buckle before
this unsung brilliance

and finally declare itself
woefully and humbly

at a loss

rosé

i'm somewhere in the middle
between a child
soothed to sugared silence
with a spoonful of calpol
and an old maid
looking down the neck
of a empty bottle
wondering where her youth went

these are the sickly sweet times
where solace comes in
the false promise of tomorrow
and a mug of cheap rosé wine
pour yourself a measure
you fleeting piece of glory
we have all the time in the world
and no time at all

pull up a chair
ferment with me

come over here

come over here
where it's dark and cosy
and even the stars fear to tread
i've got two fat handfuls of now
burning a slow mantra into my palms

i've fucking got this

i think

(i am a whole new brand of clumsy
a rubik's cube of second guesses
sliding and clashing in your
tender palms)

this time i will not hand you my body
with a thousand and one clauses
i will shut up
for once

i am here on purpose

this body once felt
like the x on someone else's
treasure hunt
but this is not a rehearsal
or an exam
grease the hinges of this night
grown light-headed from
holding its breath

come over here
where it's dark and cosy
and for whole minutes at a time
we glint like broken glass
in the corners of abandoned rooms
all our sharpness giving the
light something
to bounce off

tent

it is inadvisable
to splay your legs for a man you do not know
with hair that girls like you singe your scalps for
burnt toffee on your teeth and tongue
he will leave a residue for days
even if you wanted to
you don't get to keep him

intimacy remains a party trick
you aren't sure how to get all your
limbs back intact from
you like to be looked at
feel someone stare hungrily
until you are pressed in on both sides

a dangerous high to chase after
you know better than to chop
your body up into meat
but sometimes
you want to be eaten
for fear the rot will set in

you fill the air with incessant talk
compensating for the silence
those raw forms of communication
that branch out of the quiet

as the sunrise curdles
in the sky's open stomach
here you are
fearful
peppered with pinpricks of starlight

sometimes
you will need affirmation you are
beautiful from someone else

so believe that strange man
you invite back to your tent
when he tells you

you
are
delicious

roasted vegetables

discs of courgette and aubergine
so flavourful i ate the seconds
straight out of the saucepan

nothing but
olive oil, pepper and salt
i know because i watched you

i've tried it so many times
in my own kitchen
yet it never tastes the same

was it the brand of oil
the baking tray you used
or some other thing
you did with those hands

that i fear i'll never
be able to replicate
again?

a recipe for retaliation

you will need:

a single tongue swollen fat
from the constant muzzle of teeth

black nail polish: two coats

several cups of cheap instant coffee left to cool
a liquid seethe

the hardened instep of a flamenco dancer
the arm swing of a krumper slicing through the night

the worn-down heel of a stiletto

the grin of a golliwog

a barbed kiss

apple cores, banana peels, desiccated toast crumbs

the brittle bones of a nameless ancestry
(for best results, grind down to a fine powder)

every insincere smile bent back on itself

one furled umbrella
a generous dash of pepper spray
a rusted knuckle duster

gravel
citrus
salt

anything to make old wounds
scream afresh

method:

they have drowned women like you before and still do.
burned them at stakes and locked them in asylums for daring to speak
for not sanitising their screams
for plunging their hands below their waistbands and mining for answers.

do as you always have done. bide your time. nurse the bloodlust.

they tap you on the shoulder, lean in and whisper
i'm sorry, dear, i'm not sure you're aware but
there appears to be a fully loaded expletive between your legs.

suspicion is still in the air.
they whisper about you, stroke at your skin
as if they'd like to exhibit it on a magnolia wall.

all kinds of ways will be found to remind you stillness was meant to be your default.
your anger is ugly and will not put on its frilly party dress
won't sit with its legs crossed and laugh at all the right moments.

you've been trained to be your own leash.

the truest bits of you make you uncomfortable
make you hunt your own flesh with blunt teeth.

so when they say *calm down*

when they say *shhhh*

when they say *it's all gone a bit far, hasn't it?*

it's as if they've never listened to nina simone at 4am
and felt the fangs of apocalypse either side of their head.

like they've never watched a seven-year-old suck in her stomach.

like they've never switched on the news to a bus in delhi.

like they've never watched grown men
in dark suits write blind dogma inside our wombs.

like they have no grasp of elementary chemistry:

first it simmers
then it boils
and then it
spills over.

the skies are grey with remorse

our names pull us
at opposite ends of ourselves
souls split across the equator
skins made for certain climates
our voices shaped by another
so what britain are we to speak of?
the one that makes us feel like
we live on the head of a matchstick?

no wonder we are always
searching the seas and skies
for a sign of things to come
no wonder we british are always fearful
of leaving the house without umbrellas

and though some lovesick part of me
will always romanticise the rain
perhaps the darker truth is
the skies are grey with the remorse
history books still refuse to speak of

so please keep your hoods up
and your heads down
it doesn't look like the downpour
will cease any time soon

whore

Martin Luther King Jr is a man known for his peaceful activism during the Civil Rights Movement in the 1960s and most notably his 'I Have a Dream' speech. Coretta Scott King was his wife, with whom he had four children before his untimely murder in 1968. It is a lesser-known fact that Martin Luther King had multiple extramarital affairs, evidence of which was recorded by the FBI through hotel room bugs in an attempt to tarnish his reputation. The moral implications of this are, in this particular instance, irrelevant. Very few women have had the chance to tell their version of history. This is a poem from the perspective of one of Martin Luther King's mistresses.

he didn't speak much
this majestic man that led
a nation with his words
his gaze was mute
those big old hands clumsy

so i undressed myself
a congregation of one
god help me
i worshipped him

he'd blaspheme his way to climax
then turn his back to me
bereft and gasping
i knew better than to touch or look at him
no, i'd just lay there
silent as sin
feeling the walls' ears perk up
part of me was glad that
someone
somewhere
bore witness

he didn't like any talk of the 'movement'

that all got hushed up
brushed off like whining mosquitoes

he liked to reminisce and i liked to listen
he sure knew his way round a story
man could make me laugh
till i choked

he'd hold me close and tell me
all about his childhood days
he always wanted to play dice
with the big boys
but he was never allowed, see
those cats played for money
that was gambling and gambling
was a heathen's sport
so he learnt to amuse himself
any old how

he loved to run most of all
playing hide and seek with himself
damn near quickest feet on the block
could never outrun
the lick of his daddy's switch
though

in summer he'd lick the smoky sauce
from his fingers on cookout days
his grandma would sneak him
extra wings in greasy napkins
he'd hold 'em in his hot hands
rush to his room to eat 'em up
real fast before his mama caught him

that's me
a shameful greasy thing
he steals artless mouthfuls of
in tiny hotel rooms with cheap sheets
that bring me out in a mean old rash

could've said all this
but i didn't
i'd just stroke his head
tell him i make a mean gumbo
that one day he should try it
we both knew that day weren't coming
any time this side of never

there's a word folks like to use
for women like me
it swallows everything
in its bottomless mouth
his memory will live in glory
as it ought to
but i'll be some dirty nameless thing
recorded moans in a secret database
evidence he was just a regular old man
and i a regular old whore

so be it then

they don't know
how he came to me in tears
and i was the only one
who could put him back together
to fight another day
so in some small and godless way
i was the one
who set you all
free

cunnilingus

i'm timing you when you're down there, boy

technique and diligence are crucial factors
but more potently all the time you do
(or more crucially
don't)
spend down there is an indictment
a trophy or condemnation

you decide

it can and will be used in a court of law
as an assessment of your character

screenshots of your time sent to and dissected
by an army of vicious and incisive girlfriends
compared and contrasted with candidates past and present

intricate graphs of data correlating time spent
with political affiliation, brand of boxers worn
intensity of attachment to mothers
and indeed any other female relations

i am claiming back so many minutes
lost down the back of a sofa slouched
in a poorly lit room under a houseless roof

this is for every single time
my tongue could not travel the back alley
leading to something shaped like desire
something resembling rapturous unravel

every single time they
1) did not ask
2) did not offer
3) did not care

the clock hands shower me with rapturous applause
it has simultaneously been mere seconds
and also forever

at some point
feel free to come up for air
preferably with a poem of gratitude
held between your teeth

annual strip club massacre

the moët and chandon was flowing
atlanta beats belching from the speakers
stacey was rocking pvc and that arse was glorious
a true fuck-you to the laws of gravity
alex studded her neon pink bra by hand
and it glowed in the dark, too

it was a special night
so only the big players got an invite
the CEOs and banker boys
with cheerless wives to avoid
the type to drop two grand on a private dance
only to sit a girl on their lap for the hour
talking of the white noise in their heads

some of them were kind, of course
others were not
the usual story
handsy and entitled
thought more cash would get them
a fuck, a permanent mistress
an express ticket to the manhood
that so clearly eluded them

it was almost too easy
fiona started off by piercing
her stiletto heel into an eye socket
jess choked one to death
with his own leather belt
he'd once told her he liked
a firm hand around the neck
just before he climaxed
so there's worse ways to go

the girls turned the music up
arranged the corpses
in the chairs and booths

(kay was glad she didn't
wear her white ensemble)
it was a packed house
their favourite punters
in pride of place by the stage
eyeless heads agog
trousers slung down to the ankle
stiff fingers placed by their cocks
some still standing to attention

they put on their best show yet
writhed and twerked
ground their hips and bit their lips
cheering each other on into the early hours
another successful strip club massacre

a mutually beneficial exchange
a swan song of seamless rage
a full stop unstuck

take up space

take

up

space

don't wait for permission or approval
let go of those ghostly
question marks?
haunting the ends of your sentences
always the one
laughing at the jokes
you can make them too
not just about sex, diets or tampons
you are not the wingtip tick on a quota list
fleeting footnote on final page
decorative nod to diversity
no fucking way

take
up
space
in pink skirts or black doc martens
souls can dance unchecked
beneath the fortress of burkas
baggy t-shirts and ripped jeans
shave your legs or don't
smile from ear to ear or don't
here
a goddess of spit and sweat
stumbling in a pit of phoenix ashes

TAKE **UP** ***SPACE***

believe the compliments you are given
(bbz. ur buff. the absolute buffest)

we are indispensable

walking pillars of defiance
in every exhale of breath
assured step of foot towards threshold
the journey has been long
but now

take up

space
in any way you choose
don't wear your body
as if this sacred package of skin
nerves and blood-rush restlessness
were an accident
a graceless misstep of fate or fortune
when you hold yourself with joy and purpose
no misguided man
can ever make a wounded elegy of your flesh
you go ahead
t
a
k
e
u
p
s
o
m
e
m
o
r
e
s
p
a
c
laugh for longer and loud e r

than what’s deemed appropriate
giggles rising up to the sky

like a chorus of homesick angels

take a whole page
take a whole book

take a whole world

take

up

a recipe for retreat

you will need:

everything to fall away

method:

pretend to be a hedgehog.

how strange to spend your whole youth craving adulthood
only to get there and want nothing more than to be told:
go here, do this, eat that.
don't cry.
it will be okay.

nothing will be made today.

go back to bed.
go back to your fifteen-year-old self.
go back to where you came from.
go back to the womb.

go incognito. go zygote.

stagnate for several millennia.

reduce into a puddle of chromosome.

when finally, totally numb, serve yourself up to the fates.
fall without choreography or fanfare
arse-over-tit-over-soul-over-substance
into silence.

heirloom

in a culture where depression is
considered a western indulgence
she cannot describe the damp swarm
of nothingness that sits over her skull
the people she loves will shut her in a room
with a towel under the door
so her sadness won't permeate the air
or poison the stew

in a country where marriage
is a woman's social currency
she sits at home at midday
with the curtains closed
a beautiful weeping willow mind
descends into wasteland
as her children learn
to tread around her like a landmine

in a home where a wife
must offer her body up silently
to a husband who returns
with breath stained from
cheap beer and foreign names
the inner thighs are an unanswered prayer
the lower back a choked gasp
she hopes against hope
her children will not grow to be
the crooked sum of their conception

in a lineage of lone and wilful women
she learns to speak with flexed fists
loves her children with
a stooped back and stern words
there is no use for lingering embraces
or soft reprimands

trust is a freedom too dangerous
for her to rest her weary back against
all she has is her strength
the strength she holds aloft like a rusting chalice
her most precious heirloom
and heaviest burden

fetish

show me that deviant skin
lay it across this crisp white bed
splay yourself out
so i can see you

you glow after dark and under sheets
my acquired taste
an uncharted fork
in this straight narrow road

you remind me of my travelling days
grazing my tongue across your neck
i recall the delicious sting of foreign spices
tiling the roof of my mouth

how i bent down to take pictures
of hunched brown bodies
eating with their hands
darling, i am famished

let me name your endless wonders
a bubbling list of explorer's spoils
honey, molasses and cocoa
that sugar cane spine begging

to be split to sip
its unbearably sweet sap
darling, i am thirsty

you: this silence, this secret
this devil dance
twisted truth
inverted idyll

believe me when i say
that you are beautiful
and i am insatiable

you no longer have to be a ghost
unseen, unknown, unloved
but please don't walk over there
into that garish light

come back here
into the dark
so i can see
you

pda

couples on the tube confuse you
such propriety in how they touch
hips chiselled to the exact curve
of their partner's palms
it would seem
as they kiss
you declare a staring contest
with their undulating jaws
a sense of dread settles
and makes itself at home

you lean in by a fraction of a breath
make earnest notes
of the mouths worth melting into
and those that gape in hungry silence
us silent hordes that grow tired
of endless love affairs with loneliness
and learn to court nonchalance instead

slow jam

climbing legs-first out of minnie riperton's throat
it's safe to say the landing was traumatic
heavy-lidded eyes cowered from
the unforgiving light
a poor pickled young thing
prostrate in a pool of tepid melodies

it didn't get any easier

the truth was she felt cheated

she would forever be
a slow jam played backwards
a baby-making tune heard thinly
in an abortion clinic waiting room

needle and vinyl meet
a voice sweet enough and thick enough
to send summer back into its chrysalis

she has not heard
this particular track before
yet she finds all the words
already living under her tongue

this one's about heartbreak
this one's about loneliness

this one's for all the lovers out there

a moment of silence

After WH Auden (I finished the poem, then realised it sounded a bit like that corny poem from Four Weddings and a Funeral. *I think poetry rules state that if you put 'after so-and-so' then you're not a plagiarist. Safe).*

please no tweets
viral hashtags
or profile picture flags

sit on your thinkpieces
and counter-thinkpieces
roll the sharp tongues
back into your mouths

let the hush after the gunshot
or bomb blast ring through our ribs
we will relearn the art of being
slack and speechless

we will spend as much time
with the feeling as we do its definition
a whole minute will go by
our phones and thoughts in flight mode

we will bow before the infinite things
that soften spines and steal spirits
momentarily we will sink

resurface
and only then
let our voices take the helm
and the circus recommence

things i cannot promise you

unconditional love beauty unwavering kindness understanding
perspective forever a few years a few months tomorrow the
right words at the right time orgasms pleasure pleasantness
that i am pleasant that i am lovable that i am worthy that i am a
pause for thought that i am not a stranger that i am not an actor
that i am not a master of illusion a contortionist a magician that
i am not excellent at making things disappear

that we won't look back in five years struggle to recall surnames
smiles shared secrets that we won't be an echo of deja vu in
the next fuck buddy's nervous laughter that it won't all feel so
meaningless and fleeting that i won't run from you like a crime
scene that you won't become a blood stain i want to bleach with
my own spit

unconditional love beauty unwavering kindness understanding
perspective forever my god i could fill a forest's worth of
notebooks with all the things i cannot promise you

but know this right now i am seasick with joy and right now a
promise can only stretch so far as the length of my fingers walking
the path of your dormant spine as you sleep

this moment has a pulse and things can only die

if they were alive in the first place

a recipe for absorption

you will need:

a cold slap of water in the mornings

a change in season

a change in perspective

heavy duty walking shoes

a bird feather

a chipped sea shell

a firm grip

a steady hand

an eye for circles, figure eights and boomerangs

a broth of clarity – hot, steaming and served in a big white bowl

method:

fear for the day when you stop wanting to peel back the curtain and watch the cogs at work.

the small things humble you with how light a touch they have. a poignancy that does not announce itself but settles somewhere just on the periphery. the coral of a new nail polish could bring you to tears one day – could be the one thing holding your universe together. you take the time to let it dry.

all things have their time.

pigeons with missing claws will hobble past you like soothsayers – it's all you can do not to call out to them in public, ask them to spare you a story, an ancient proverb, some stray crumb of wisdom. the rhythmic jackhammer of their heads amuses you, touches something deep in the gourd of your chest. you have tried and failed to express this to people and it is an honour to still be rendered speechless.

there will be a bleakness that will seem to cling to even the most glorious of landscapes. it will announce itself with a pompous grandeur, demand pride of place at the table.

you don't have to indulge this. it can sit in the chair assigned to it, no higher or lower than any other guests.

look and look and
look again.

take your armbands off. you can and will float.

if you suspect it's not that deep, entertain the notion that

maybe

just maybe

it's not that deep

and if it were

surely you'd have sunk by now?

how to raise a man

prise him open
gently
point out the crucial parts
heart, pelvis, liver, spine discs fragile as biscuit
punchbag lungs
show him where the salt collects
the hiding places where hurt often finds its home
teach him what restlessness looks like
so he recognises the whirlpools
it will make in the gutter of his stomach

encourage him to be a sailor
a conductor of the sea of selfhood
and its wistful symphonies
chew at your knuckles
knead the doughy stem of your neck
weary from craning over your shoulder
get used to short, shallow stabs of breath
breaking out of your mouth
in stilted staccato

keep offering him the balm of your smile
show him how to plant laughter like seeds in soil
lament the day others show him
how to fling it across front lines like grenades
lose count of the years that have gone by
since you've seen him cry
he is not granted permission
to cave in on himself
so be his cave

keep him safe when he allows himself
to soften under your gaze
this is immeasurably hard for him
but still
prise him open once more
roll your sleeves up

cower at the stranger wearing your eyes
mourn the little boy who built kingdoms with k'nex
slip handwritten notes into his battered trainers
never stop showing him he is worth writing poems for
though you fear one day
you will be writing eulogies
swallow your fear
swallow your hope
delete as appropriate

prise him open again
kiss the scar tissue
suppress the urge to scream
into the aching cavity of him
assure him the protein shakes and dumbbells
cannot, will not, will never
make him strong enough to lift the weight
of things to come from off his shoulders
rewrite the dictionary for him
redefine power, honour, struggle
legacy

your fingers will tremble
do not let them
bargain with whatever deities will listen
show him touch has nothing to do with ownership
clasp his hands together
will the learned violence out of them
place his fingers on your stomach
the haven where he was once
just a bundle of best intentions
remind him he is a genetic miracle
refuse to let him use his eyes
fists or dick as weapons

trust him
learn him, unlearn him
and learn him again
when you hate him
love him instead

tenderness is not an easy gift to extend
it is dogged, bloody and relentless
prise him open one last time

step back

this is what a man is made of

battle rap boys

i have seen unlikely angels before
flat caps casting shadows over
constellations of spots and stubble

they bray and holler and slap their chests
boast of shooting guns, breaking jaws
voraciously fucking each other's mothers

fifty fellas to every girl in these
sweat dens where the grime is loud
and the quiet fear i felt profound

here they rewrite themselves
as back alley mythology
wear the rage of vengeful gods

but after the camera cuts
the statuesque swag deflates
they no longer fill their xl t-shirts

they speak fondly of young daughters
offer smiles acquainted with kindness
and my heart softens to the scene

reformed loners turned foul-mouthed prophets
their holy book spat in sixteen-bar format
you have never seen anything as tender

as a pulsing mob of men roar for each other
revelling in the bloodsport of boyhood
before piecing each other back again

overpriced pints disappear down throats
as they offer up their brutal words
like fresh bruises to be appraised

numbed
or nursed
as necessary

living room worship

though you are sat
alone in a private
cocoon of grace
i've never felt closer to you

it is still humbling
watching you pray
to a god that slipped
from my shoulders
one unremarkable night

(and though i miss him
i never went looking for him again)

your eyes close
as he smooths the worry lines
from your face
and i am grateful

an amen glides from your lips
just before your eyes open
to meet the room again
an awful hush descends

in the absence of mercy
in the absence of faith
in the absence of
any other respite

i will pray with you

lumidee

If weather permits, go and read this poem outside. If it's a blisteringly hot summer's day, so much the better. Play 'Never Leave You (Uh Ooh)' by Lumidee at full volume, preferably the far superior remix with Busta Rhymes and Fabolous.

you have to have been there
but basically
it was all beginning

i had a new top from tammy girl
the kind of top you can't wait to wear
on home clothes day
a top you mourn each minute
it sits in the laundry basket

for the first time i realised
summer was a feeling
where everyone
remembers their skin
like a once-loved party dress
patiently waiting for an invite
to hit the doormat

it was all beginning

but back to that top
with betty boop pouting on the front
studded with sassy diamante scripture
drawstrings on either side revealing
the fresh-from-the-oven muffin top
pubescence had gifted you
that perfect lumidee beat
persistently uppercutting the air
every song on the radio
was an ode to what a woman's hips can do

my beautiful top would soon be
jaundiced with sweat stains
an aunt took me aside and told me
i'd have to shave under my arms
to wear such things in public
lumidee turned out to be
a reedy-voiced one-hit wonder
never to pierce the charts again

but man
for a moment
it was all beginning
basically
you have to have been there

transit

when you've concertinaed yourself
into this many train, plane, bus and coach seats
even when you stretch out
you're all crinkle and yawn
hand-me-down road rage

travelling through the world's intestines
it shows you all its perversions
the stories and dilemmas it struggles to digest
somewhere along the journey
metaphors become the wilful lies
that get you through the fluoro-tinted night
climb aboard, climb aboard
your exits are here, here and
where?

finally
you lie still in a house you pay hundreds
to feel a much sought for solace
yet all you can dream of are
endless roads
unfolding like shed snakeskins
your unease hisses you
into the nearest approximation of sleep

holiday

on a crack of dawn flight
to another country, another tongue
and another culture
you are tired of the crick in your neck
the press of the seat in front of your knees

you want to be stationary
greeted by the same view from your window
for at least three consecutive days

but when you land
you are met with the joy
of unfamiliar streets and universal customs
a myriad of words for *hello*, *thank you* and *sorry*
are brief guests in your bashful mouth

as you walk round a grand fountain
framed in the dazzling green only
the utopia of scandinavia could offer
a conversation with an aunt
floats to the top of your mind

one in which she confided
she had never left her country
that all her other siblings had
never even left their village

and it's all you can do
not to weep in the face of chance
and its callous scattergun hand
you vow to never take the miracle
of flight for granted again
but the tears do not stop

a kind fair-haired man stops
to survey the scene of you
and before you can look away
he asks in improbably perfect english
if there's anything he can do
to help you

a recipe for release

you will need:

that niggling thing

you know the one

illegally squatting at the top of your spine

the monsters still hosting illegal

raves under your bed and behind your

eyelids

the thwack-bump-thwack

of the past and present bare-knuckle

fighting outside a wetherspoon's

ten signs the end of the world is coming

eleven ways to send it off in style

the best pop song ever

anything and everything that reflects the light

a scatter of pomegranate seeds

gaudy earrings

autumn-tinged puddles

the fleshy ripple of scar tissue

the underside of the first cd you ever bought

the saliva you spit-shone it with

a childhood serving of body glitter

anything and EVERYTHING that reflects the light

the orphaned words you deemed unworthy of poetry

that pneumatic drill mouth of yours

the sheets of static draped across the windows

all the chaos, peeled and chopped into bitesize chunks

method:

on the count of three

1

2

not worth shaving your arsehole for

just not worth shaving your arsehole for
if it isn't urgent, a geyser in your naughty parts
a party in your pants
if he isn't making you feel reminiscent
of the first crush you wanted to smush
your training-braed chest against

get your hands out his novelty boxers
get your arse out his poky bedroom
because it's not worth shaving your arsehole for

if he doesn't open doors in your mind
he won't open any revelations between your legs

if it's happening
and he's grunting and groaning away
slurring nonsense in your ear
paraphrases of drake lyrics and
stuff he's pinched from pornhub
and you're planning a grocery list in your head
transfixed by a small dark stain on the carpet
is that wine
is that blood
is it over
is it *over*

if he's looking at your body all sloppy
like you're a two-for-five-pounds frozen pizza deal
then trust me
it wasn't worth squatting over the bath
bic razor in your hand
one eye closed and tongue stuck out
the crassest of bathroom ballets
not even close

not worth that stress
that reckless rectum russian roulette
the moment when you catch yourself
in the mirror
harrowed and bumbling
a delayed punchline to a terrible joke

don't do it to yourself

if he doesn't know where the clit is
can't even gps the damn thing
if you're lying there suppressing the urge
to burst into convulsive giggles
or hot volcanic tears
then it's
just
not
worth
it
is it?

'cause when it's worth it, you'll know
and when it's worth it
your hairy arsehole
won't even matter

we don't do beyoncé

oh, you don't do beyoncé
i get it, yeah, yeah
no, don't go to too much trouble
you have wifi and a search bar
but no, you don't do beyoncé
all that pop r&b hybrid shit
capitalist canned beat autotune shit
clap clap bounce clap bounce clap shit
popular, obvious, oh-everyone-knows-it-so-it-must-be-shit
shit

you're a dj and not a jukebox
it's an integrity thing
she just wouldn't mix with this
minimal electro house
that's clearly got the crowd going

(home)

but no, no, no, no
you don't do beyoncé
it's an education thing
showing us CHILDREN
us MINIONS
us SLAVES TO THE MAINSTREAM
what real music is
surely the setting for this lesson
in forced eclecticism, isn't it
since we're here at a cheesy gay bar
in the sweaty arse crack of a tuesday night
me and my two mates the only
upright people left on the dancefloor

we just want to be soulless
pop-loving automatons for once
to be mindless and limbless
spinning around like sugar threads
in a candyfloss machine
like independent women

like bootylicious, like grown women
like burst chrysalis, like burnt sugar
like a long tall tart glass of lemonade
like beauty, like power, like fun

do you remember when music was *fun* for you
not a game of one-upmanship
a competition or thorn in your throat
a way of dividing people up
into worthy and worthless

when did it come to this?
i'm sorry that people pay fifty quid to watch
calvin harris press some buttons at fabric
while these fuckers barely covered your travel
i'm sorry your faultless vinyl collection
collects dust and grudges in your garage
i'm sorry your club night failed
that your partner left you
and you had to move back in with your parents

i'm sorry it doesn't sound like it used to
that the party came to an end for you
long before everyone else was ready to leave
i'm sorry this thing that once kept you sane
now eats you alive
mate, this life's done a number on all of us

but just this once
you can stop defining yourself
by what you don't do
put on something to get us dancing
some cheesy chart shit to help
our hearts sit and swell to their full size

he looks me in the eyes
and with a mirthless sigh says:

sorry
no
we don't do beyoncé

mantra

if it doesn’t feel better after a wank and a biscuit

reassess

cackle

i do not fear much
having prepared myself
for the fact that all things must end
and no life is free from heartache

but i'm certain
i am mostly held together
with the many moments we have
shattered into cackles on
our shitty second-hand sofas

the days we have made
witty folklore of the sorest parts
of us, convinced our mishaps
would make the best sitcom
to ever grace the telly

i don't care if some boy
never texts me again
or if i wake up with a head
forever empty of poems

only the thought of drifting from you
makes the world truly strange and sad
a shitty armchair for one
a cackle leaping out of my mouth
with no echo to meet it

drown

once again they placed rocks in your pockets
and challenged you to walk on water

it was a joke only you and the shore shared
how could the ocean ever swallow you

when your womb is rocked to sleep
by the gentle pull of the moon

who in turn knows and owns the tides
that your ancestors bathed and worshipped in

your saboteurs did not know where to look
as you advised they sought another cautionary tale

you have no intention of suffering
for anyone's salvation except your own

last night

1. the bedroom

a bitter mid-november night   bare legs exposed 'cause black tights won't go with the playsuit   the hem flirts a little too hard with your arsecheeks   but the pattern is so pretty   and the way it cinches your waist   feels like a first dance

2. the alcohol run

thin wad of notes in a balled fist   a litre of gin split three ways   at some point we stopped keeping tabs on who owes who   one gets the pre-drinks   the other the uber   the third the dutty chips at 3am

3. the queue

political chats are happening behind you   your mates slur and slice through an agenda of world crises   whilst you are transfixed by the forearms of the man in front of you   his shirt sleeves rolled to just above the elbow   tensing and releasing like a bass player teasing a funky riff from taut strings   a desperate croak sneaks out of you
you alright, hun?
unconvincingly   you turn the croak into a coughing fit   your friend slaps your back   her eyes slant and soften in genuine concern

4. the bouncer

sometimes you forget you're a grown-ass woman   who fills out tax returns and owns a vase   you grin the grin of a shit liar   as the bouncer's narrowed eyes dart from your passport photo to you and back again   it still feels like a triumph   every time they wave you in to the belly of the beast

5. the bar

honestly what is money even for if you cannot buy a round of
drinks for your best friends in the whole entire world and the girl
with the deep wine-coloured lipstick that you've just met whose
name is mary or mandy or perhaps harriet golden oceans
with islands of jäger in the middle down in one your hearts
immediately start beating at 160 bpm

6. the toilets

music bleeds down the passageway we two step in time squeezing
pelvic floors to keep from pissing ourselves under a cubicle door a
tampon is passed to a grateful hand strangers call each other babe,
love and pumpkin absentmindedly a woman lifts her top to stroke
a caesarean scar you can take a few minutes to fall apart in here
no questions asked the code of conduct is watertight everyone is
beautiful do not answer that text be a love and guard the door
with the broken lock whilst excess is expelled down a long-suffering
toilet bowl

7. the smoking area

takes a few moments to adjust to the fact that we don't have to
shout to be heard out here perhaps we prefer the forced intimacy of
having to lean in to each other in the loud and dark the licence to
touch and linger longer than british etiquette allows

8. the dancefloor

if you didn't already know we're not here to fuck about hair
tied back away from our necks shorts worn tight to our hips an
airhorn call to duty summons us find us dangerously close to the
speakers where the throb and wobble reigns dextrous waists wine
up against any man who can keep up
hands rest on bent knees small of back pops and twists asking and
answering the same question we dip and sway salute with barrel
fingers yes mate yes sweat collects between and under breasts

thin cotton tops damp to the touch   dj drops banger after banger
vicious   a delicious ache in the pelvis   we   bubble butterfly   tick
tock   hands press against the wall   all the better to throw it back
we make it clap   turn it up   reload that   somehow we have
formed a tight circle   moving with and for each other   bending
and refracting   let's go let's go let's go   chants spread and pitch to a
euphoric crescendo   when the last song ends and the lights come up
we blink dumbstruck   the floor beneath us sticks   the sweat on our
skin dries to a quiet itch

9.   the walk back

with takeaway boxes sploshed with a palette of miscellaneous sauces
we debrief on the night's shenanigans   eyes wide but unfocused
words slow to assemble in succinct order   some nights we return with
bodies brimful of catharsis   others we are cowering from the demons
that only come out under strobe lights   regardless   there has never
been a night we haven't made it back   pint glasses of tap water
perched on bedside tables   another day forces its way through the
windows   we often don't make it into our own rooms   falling into
fitful sleep on one bed   a tangle of hair and hope and   dormant
hunger

acknowledgements

Mum and Dad for making me. More specifically, Dad for praising me and Mum for raising me.

Burning Eye for publishing me twice, dealing with my scattiness with grace and patience and especial thanks to Clive for your support and kindness in times of artistic and/or financial strife.

Sam Thomas. You're right. You are an angel. I love you.

To the women who inspire me, support me, challenge me, champion me, listen to me, tolerate me, love me and accept me for everything that I am:

Kav the Wifey, Tash, Mim, Sarah, Francie, Hollie McNish, Rebecca Tantony, Joelle Taylor, Deborah Stevenson, Sherony Lock (thank you for the gorgeous cover), Ngaio Aniya, Charlotte Spires and my lovely agent Becky Thomas. I also extend this to every woman I've ever stayed up all night with, cooked brunch for, swapped sex tips with and offered secrets to (there are many more of you I could name who I see far too little but love dearly, but there's only so much ink and paper in this world).

To the following women whom I have never met but am indebted to for their art, their voices and their influence on me:

The Spice Girls, Destiny's Child, Nina Simone, Skunk Anansie, Whitney Houston, Chaka Khan, Lauryn Hill, Cardi B, Grace Jones, Janelle Monáe, Janet Jackson, Etta James, Leikeli47, TLC, Anita Baker, Peaches, Missy Elliott, Solange and her lesser-known sister.

To Zadie Smith, Chimamanda Ngozi Adichie, Audre Lorde, Warsan Shire, Margaret Atwood and Malorie Blackman.

To every black and brown girl everywhere.

To you holding this book.

Thank you, thank you, thank you.